What If

A METEOR HIT THE EARTH?

The Real Deal on Space Disasters —from the Experts!

Scholastic Inc.

Front cover: Andrea Danti/ Shutterstock; 1: European Space Agency; 2 top left: Mopic/ Shutterstock; 3 bottom right: Universal Images Group Getty Images; 4 Center: Henning Dalhoff/ Science Photo Library/ Getty Images; 5 bottom right: Martin Land / Science Source; 5 center right: NASA; 6: Gwen Shockey / Science Source; 7 Top left: P.Carril/ ESA; 7 bottom right: Victore Mabbick Visions/ Science Source; 8: © Boscorelli./ Alamy; 9 top left: © Dale O'Dell / Alamy; 9 bottom right: Thierry Berrod, Mona Lisa Production / Science Source; 10: Dr. Seth Shostak / Science Source; 11 center right: NASA/ AP Photo; 11 bottom left: Science Picture Co/ Getty Images; 12 center: Caspar Benson/ Getty Images; 13 top right: NASA; 13 center left: NASA; 13 bottom right: NASA; 14: iLexx/ Getty Images; 15: NASA; 16: Victor Habbick/ Visuals Unlimited; 17 top right: Boris Rabtsevich/ Shutterstock; 17 center left: NASA; 17 bottom right: Mark Williamson / Science Source; 18 center: Victor Habbick/ Visuals Unlimited/ Getty Images; 19 center left: Victor De Schwanberg/SPL/ Getty Images; 19 center right: NASA- digital version copyright /Science Faction/Corbis; 19 bottom: iLexx/ Getty Images; 20: Christian Miller/ Getty Images; 21 center: DVARG/ Shutterstock; 21 bottom right: koya979/ Shutterstock; 22 center: John T Takai/ Shutterstock; 23 top: Science Picture Co/ Getty Images; 23 right: JPL/ NASA; 23 bottom: Monica Schroeder / Science Source; 24 background: Victor de Schwanberg / Science Source; 24 center: glenda/ Shutterstock; 25 center left: NASA; 25 bottom right: Pavel Ignatov/ Shutterstock; 26 bottom right: NASA; 26: Pavel Ignatov; 27 top right: L. Calçada/M. Kornmesser/European Southern Obvservatory; 27 center: M. Kornmesser/ European Southern Observatory; 28 center: Walter Myers / Science Source; 29 top right: JPL/ NASA; 29 center right: Friedrich Saurer / Science Source; 29 bottom right: European Space Agency / DLR / FU Berlin / G. Neukum / Science Source; 30 top right: Victor Habbick Visions/ Science Photo Library; 30 bottom left: Walter Myers / Science Source; 31 top right: Aaron Rutten/ Shutterstock; 31 bottom right: NASA.

ISBN 978-0-545-50836-0

12 11 10 9 8 7 6 5 4 3 2 1   13 14 15 16 17 18/0

Printed and assembled in China

First printing, February 2014

CONTENTS:

Space is a huge place. Earth is just one tiny planet. Who knows what's out there? The possibilities for catastrophe are plentiful— and so much fun to explore! Get ready to meet some leading experts who will tackle these hair-raising questions:

What If a Meteor Hit the Earth? · **4**

What If Aliens Invaded Your Town? · **8**

What If Your Spacecraft Lost Contact with Mission Control? · **12**

What If Space Junk Started Raining Down on Earth? · · · · · · · · · · **16**

What If the Sun Stopped Shining? · · · · · · · · · · · · · · · · · · · **20**

What If You Got Sucked into a Black Hole? · · · · · · · · · · · · · · · **24**

What If You Were Stranded on Mars? · · · · · · · · · · · · · · · · · · **28**

As you read, you will come across words in bold. If you don't know the meaning, look it up in the glossary on page 32.

WHAT IF A METEOR HIT THE EARTH?

A huge space rock zooms toward the planet and enters Earth's atmosphere, burning brightly in the sky. Could this meteor annihilate Earth?

WHAT'S A METEOR?

Meteors start out as **asteroids**. So, let's start with "what's an asteroid?" Scientists believe that 4.6 billion years ago (before our solar system was born) there was just a rotating disk of gas and dust. The central, superhot, spinning ball of gas formed the sun. The particles clumped together and grew, forming the planets in the solar system. There are some leftover chunks, and these are called asteroids.

Where can you find asteroids? Some roam around in near-Earth space. But most hang out far from Earth. About a million asteroids hover between Jupiter and Mars. This rock-filled region is called the main asteroid belt.

he main belt is like an action-packed obstacle course. Asteroids constantly smash into one another. Colliding space rocks can cause a whole asteroid or pieces of one to rocket toward Earth. Yes, asteroids can fall out of the sky!

Every day, about 100 tons of space debris bombard Earth's atmosphere. These small pieces of asteroids are called **meteoroids**, and are usually dust- to pebble-size. When the particles rub against the air molecules that make up Earth's atmosphere, **friction** occurs. This causes the rocky material to heat up and burn as a meteor.

Every few weeks, bigger pieces of asteroids—ranging in size from a baseball to a small car—enter the atmosphere. These larger pieces burn brighter and longer than meteors, and are called fireballs.

If a meteor doesn't burn up completely, it can land on Earth. It becomes known as a **meteorite**.

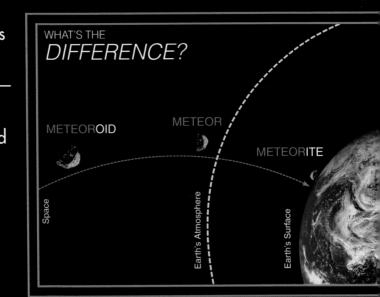

WHAT'S THE
DIFFERENCE?

METEOROID

METEOR

METEORITE

Space

Earth's Atmosphere

Earth's Surface

◆ WHAT ABOUT TEKTITE? ◆

When a meteorite hits the Earth, it can cause parts of the ground to melt and splash upward. When this material falls back down, it cools into glassy tektites. Just like the one that came with this book!

WHAT ARE THE CHANCES?

The chances of a meteor hitting the Earth are 100 percent—it has happened before, and it WILL happen again!

COULD THIS REALLY HAPPEN?

NO WAY · HIGHLY UNLIKELY · MAYBE · **ABSOLUTELY**
?

Every few hundred years, a sizable meteorite can cause some local damage. For example: On February 15, 2013, a school-bus-size asteroid exploded into a fireball over the Ural region in Russia. It broke into many pieces of meteorites. The shock from the explosion, along with the scattering of debris, caused injuries to more than 1,500 people.

mpact crater. The worst smash-up occurred about 65 million years ago. The crash occurred n present-day Mexico. Scientists believe the hit kicked up so much dust, it blocked sunlight. Result: Without sunlight, many plants died. This killed large animals (including the dinosaurs) that depended on plants for food.

But Don't Panic!

There's no need to hit the panic button just yet. Dangerous meteorites are rare and would only affect a small area. The chances of wide-scale global damage are pretty unlikely. Just ask an expert!

DOOMSDAY?

Reports of Earth being crushed by a mammoth asteroid pop up every so often. "Much of it is nonsense!" says Dr. Don Yeomans, planetary scientist at NASA Jet Propulsion Laboratory. His team uses powerful telescopes to track the positions of potentially dangerous asteroids. They also use radar to measure their size, speed, and distance. These calculations help compute the path an asteroid may take over the next hundred or so years. Findings show that Earth is under no threat of complete destruction.

Knock It Off: Even if Earth is not on a collision course, scientists are thinking ahead. They're devising ways to deal with potential runaway rocks. One idea is to get a spacecraft to nudge it away from Earth. Another idea would be to blow up the asteroid. So far, no government agency has been asked to build these deflectors or destroyers. For now, NASA is focusing on getting higher-quality telescopes. This would help Yeomans's team better patrol the skies.

WHAT IF ALIENS INVADED YOUR TOWN?

If you believe what you see in the movies, aliens are pretty strange. What if they exist and tried to take over?

COULD THIS REALLY HAPPEN?

NO WAY   HIGHLY UNLIKELY   **MAYBE**   ABSOLUTELY

?

"We don't know if aliens exist. It's a question we've been asking for millennia (thousands of years), and we still don't have an answer. The very first scientific paper on SETI was written in 1959. The last sentence said, 'The probability of success is difficult to estimate; but if we never search the chance of success is zero.' So we're trying to search and explore in a systematic way to see if we can find the answer."

—Dr. Jill Tarter, Astronomer, SETI (Search for Extraterrestrial Intelligence) Institute, Mountain View, California

A HUMAN'S GUIDE TO ALIENS

SETI scientists, including Tarter, believe that it is possible for aliens to exist. That's because space is enormous. There are billions of **stars** and planets in our **galaxy** that are many times older than Earth. If Earth can host life, other places might, too!

No one knows what an alien looks like. "On Earth it makes sense to have your smarts in one place in your body," says Tarter. "Who knows what a brain would be like in an alien species?" Maybe extraterrestrials, or alien life-forms, are extra brainy and need two or more heads to operate technologies far more advanced than your laptop!

SETI scientists suspect some aliens could resemble **microbes**. Why? Because microbial life on Earth has proven that it can live in extreme environments. Some planets are far colder or warmer than Earth. Both are difficult conditions for large-scale life, as we know it, to survive. Scientists have found microbes that are well adapted to live in Earth's scorching deserts and frigid poles. By studying these extremophiles—life-forms that thrive in extreme conditions—scientists hope to gain clues on where to seek alien life.

Dr. Jill Tarter focuses her search on intelligent life in the **universe**; that means aliens capable of reasoning. How? SETI uses forty-two radio telescopes pointed toward the sky. These dish-like instruments "listen" for radio waves. These invisible waves travel very quickly through space. They are the same waves that transmit programs from a TV station to your TV.

Tarter suggests that advanced civilizations on other planets may be generating radio waves, too. The telescopes receive thousands of radio signals every day. A cluster of computers help scientists analyze the information in the detected signals to see if they are alien.

ALIEN HOT SPOT?

Space is huge, so where might be good spots to zero in on the search for aliens? In 2009, NASA launched the Kepler telescope to find exoplanets (these are planets beyond the solar system; they orbit a star other than our sun). So far, it has spied thousands of them! Some of these planets may have liquid water, as well as temperatures and an atmosphere that could support life.

◆ UPDATE ◆

After positively identifying 150 confirmed planets and more than 3,500 unconfirmed, but possible, candidates for sustaining life, in August of 2013, NASA announced that they were unable to repair some broken parts on the telescope. This doesn't mean they'll stop searching for life in space, though. Scientists are now working on creating a new mission for Kepler, using its operational parts.

Close Encounters: Imagine if, one day, SETI scientists did hear from aliens. They'd double-check their data with other scientists to make sure it wasn't a practical joke or caused by a computer malfunction. "We've had a handful of false positives (or false alarms)," says Tarter.

"But it's very exciting for a while when it happens." If the contact is genuine, "We would hold a press conference and tell the world," says Tarter.

"But we wouldn't reply until there was some sort of agreement from people around the world on whether we should. And if we do, who should speak for Earth, and what should they say." As for communicating with aliens, English wouldn't be their first language. Scientists would probably cook up a simple communication code based on math or use pictures.

WHAT IF YOUR SPACECRAFT LOST CONTACT WITH MISSION CONTROL?

An astronaut aboard a spacecraft radios the crew on Earth for instructions. Oops. No sound. What now?

COULD THIS REALLY HAPPEN?

NO WAY   HIGHLY UNLIKELY   MAYBE   **ABSOLUTELY**

?

"It could happen, and it has happened. Losing contact with the crew on board can be caused by anything. The problem could be a failure with a piece of equipment on the ground. It could be a failure with one of our satellites or even something aboard the spacecraft."

—Jacqulyne Trahan, Ground Controller, Mission Control
NASA Johnson Space Center in Houston, Texas

WAY-OUT FACTS ABOUT MISSION CONTROL

The International Space Station (ISS) hovers 250 miles (402 kilometers) above Earth. It also whizzes around the planet at 17,500 miles (28,000 km) per hour. This ride is wilder than any roller coaster on Earth.

As many as six astronauts at a time can live and work on this far-out speed machine. So NASA needs to keep tabs on the crew to make sure they are safe. This job belongs to the flight controllers at NASA Mission Control. They work round-the-clock shifts to keep in touch with the astronauts.

What's there to talk about? Every weekday, Mission Control goes through the astronauts' schedule. This includes all of their activities, from conducting experiments to the crew's schedule.

The flight controllers also check to make sure the spacecraft is operating smoothly. They help plan deliveries of fuel, food, and other supplies. The only time Mission Control is not actively watching and listening to the astronauts is during the crew's bedtime. But the Earth crew is on hand to respond to any calls.

Keeping in touch with the astronauts requires more than just picking up a phone. The ground controller is a type of flight controller who oversees and coordinates all the communications equipment that is not onboard the space station. That means monitoring hundreds of computers, video monitors, and communications satellites.

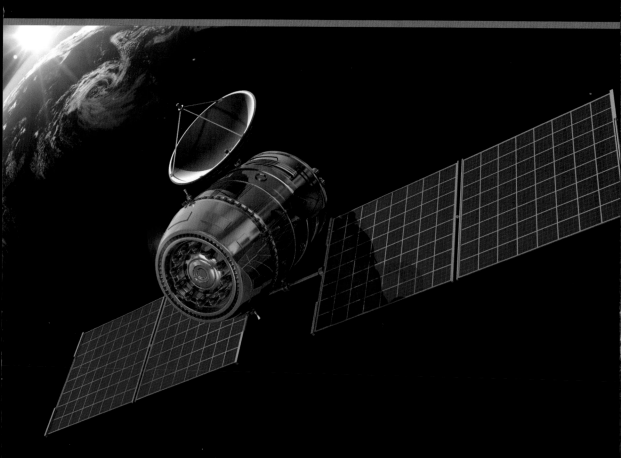

A temporary loss of communication can happen at any time, says Trahan. What's one sign that there's a breakdown? Simply that Mission Control can't send out or receive sound from the astronauts.

If the problem is on the ISS, the crew will zero in on it and try to fix it. Since astronauts can't dial in a repairman, they are trained to repair everything on board. They are prepared to deal with anything ranging from busted computers to wonky space toilets.

Sometimes, the problem is not at Mission Control or on the ISS. A communications satellite could be down. "It's not like one falling out of the sky," says Trahan. "Sometimes, a satellite experiences emergency time-outs." Basically, it just stops communicating with the ground equipment that's controlling it. It's similar to when your cell phone loses reception. Usually, a systems reboot gets the satellite up and working again.

HOUSTON, WE HAVE A PROBLEM

In 2012, however, there was a hair-raising situation with the ISS. For nearly nine hours, "We weren't able to communicate with the astronauts, but we could hear them," says Trahan. Because of this one-way communication, Mission Control wasn't able to send any commands to control the ISS. It turned out to be a timing issue with some equipment on the ground. Once the equipment synced up with others, things went back to normal. Phew!

Talking Heads: Since lots of people work at Mission Control, one person is designated to speak to the astronauts. This job belongs to the capsule communicator (CAPCOM for short). If the CAPCOM is not available, the flight director takes over. This is the team leader at Mission Control — the person responsible for the safety and success of the mission.

WHAT IF SPACE JUNK STARTED RAINING DOWN ON EARTH?

The sky above you is littered with old spacecraft and rocket parts. Any need to yell "Look out below"?

COULD THIS REALLY HAPPEN?

NO WAY   HIGHLY UNLIKELY   MAYBE   **ABSOLUTELY**
?

"A piece of space junk falls to Earth on average once a day. Many are small fragments of spacecraft or rocket bodies, weighing only a few pounds or less. However, once a week, an intact spacecraft or rocket body, weighing up to several tons, survives the fiery reentry into Earth's atmosphere."

—Dr. Nicholas L. Johnson, Chief Scientist for NASA's Orbital Debris Program, NASA's Johnson Space Center in Houston, Texas

A BRIEF, MESSY HISTORY OF SPACE JUNK

It's crowded in near-Earth space. Tools dropped by astronauts whoosh past chunks of leftover spacecraft every day. But it wasn't always this way.

Space exploration began in the 1950s. Back then, humans thought that space was so big, leaving objects up there was no big deal. Now, space is congested with human-made clutter. How much junk is up there? Millions of pieces!

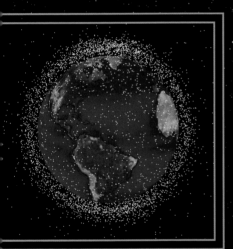

About 20,000 chunks are larger than softballs. Among these are some hefty, old spacecraft. The largest is the 10-ton *Cosmos* satellite. The Russians sent it to orbit the moon in 1970.

Next step down in size are about 500,000 pieces between the size of a softball and a marble. Paint specks and other small particles make up the rest of the space litter.

ANCIENT RELIC

The oldest piece of junk in orbit is *Vanguard 1*. The United States launched this test satellite in 1958.

PILEUP

With millions of pieces of space junk orbiting Earth, accidents will happen. In 2009, an "out of order" Russian military satellite launched in 1993 slammed into a working US telecommunications satellite. This was the first time two whole spacecraft collided. The result: They broke into more than 2,000 chunks.

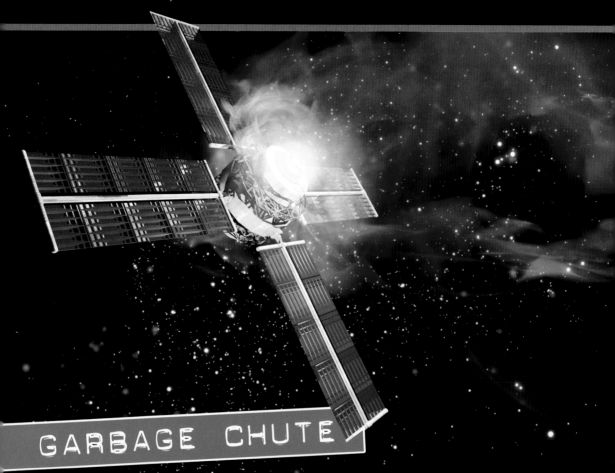

GARBAGE CHUTE

Space junk whizzes around the planet at about 17,500 miles (28,000 km) per hour. That's fast. But sometimes, that's not fast enough to escape the tug of Earth's **gravity**. Plunk!

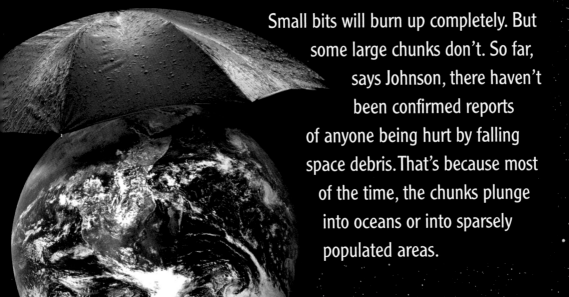

As space junk falls toward the ground, it rubs against Earth's atmosphere. Just like what you read about meteors on page 5, the junk burns up. The temperature can reach thousands of degrees!

Small bits will burn up completely. But some large chunks don't. So far, says Johnson, there haven't been confirmed reports of anyone being hurt by falling space debris. That's because most of the time, the chunks plunge into oceans or into sparsely populated areas.

TRASH PATROL

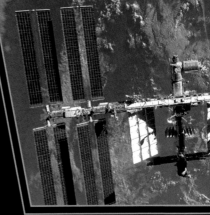

In the meantime, Johnson's team uses various ways to keep an eye on space junk. They use the US Space Surveillance Network to help track more than 22,000 human-made objects. These specific ones are 10 centimeters or larger and orbit Earth. This includes both working spacecraft and junk parts. They warn NASA whenever there is a potential run-in. "The space station maneuvers once a year to avoid being struck by a large object," says Johnson.

WHAT IF THE SUN STOPPED SHINING?

The sun provides Earth with heat and light. That's a tough job. Would it ever take a vacation and chill out?

COULD THIS REALLY HAPPEN?

NO WAY   HIGHLY UNLIKELY   MAYBE   **ABSOLUTELY**

?

"At some point, the sun will run out of fuel. The sun is almost five billion years old, halfway through its normal life, and it has enough fuel to last five billion more years."

—Dr. Todd Hoeksema, Solar Physicist, Stanford University in Palo Alto, California

LIFE WITHOUT SUNSHINE

Okay, so you know that the sun has a long life ahead. But suppose it did quit shining suddenly—like, *tomorrow*? "It would be a pretty grim scenario," says Hoeksema. It would get cold and dark right away. Earth would freeze. Nothing would survive. (Remember what happened to the dinosaurs on page 7?) Fortunately, Hoeksema asserts, "The chance of this happening is zero."

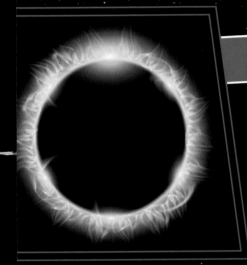

DEATH STAR

Like humans, the sun will age and slow down. What happens when the sun runs out of fuel in five billion years? It will become a red giant. This elderly star will swell to one hundred times its size. Its surface will cool to 3,600 degrees Fahrenheit (2,000°C).

A bigger sun that is closer to Earth spells doom. The heat will be so intense that the oceans will boil away. Anything left on the planet will fry. But that's not the end.

The sun's red giant phase will last millions of years. The sun will later become a white dwarf. During this final stage, the dead star will contract. It will scrunch up until it is only slightly larger than Earth. The remaining heat inside the sun will allow it to flicker for billions of years. But no one on Earth will be alive to experience it.

SIZZLING FACTS

The sun is a super star. That's right. A star. The center of our solar system started out as a giant spinning cloud of hot gas and dust. As gravity pulled the heated particles inward, the star grew larger and hotter.

Today, the sun is 865,000 miles (1,392,000 km) wide. About 1.3 million Earths could fit inside it. It is also a bright, bubbling ball of energy. The sun produces so much energy it is like a massive power station. Let's peek inside.

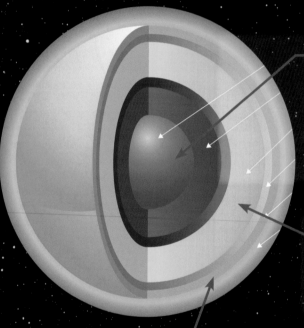

Core

Here it's a scorching 27 million degrees Fahrenheit (15 million °C)! It contains superhot particles of hydrogen. When the particles smash into one another, they produce a massive amount of energy.

Convective Zone

This layer carries the sun's energy from the core to its surface. It takes tens of thousands of years for the sun's energy to work its way up top.

Photosphere

The sun's surface emits heat and light. The temperature here is about 10,000 degrees Fahrenheit (5,500°C). Even though the sun is 93 million miles away from Earth, it takes a little more than eight minutes for sun rays to travel over.

◆ SOLAR CENTRAL ◆

Some planets get more heat and light than others. That depends on each planet's distance from the sun. For example, if you lived on Mercury, the closest planet to the sun, you'd be toast. Daytime temperatures there can reach 870 degrees Fahrenheit (465°C)! Lucky for Earth, "It's not too close or too far away," says Hoeksema.

WARM IT UP

Heat and light from the sun make life on Earth possible. Here's how solar radiation warms the planet.

1. SOLAR ENERGY HITS THE PLANET.

2. EARTH'S SURFACE ABSORBS SOME OF THE RADIATION. BUT SOME RADIATES BACK INTO SPACE.

3. SOME ENERGY HITS THE ATMOSPHERE.

4. SOME GASES IN THE ATMOSPHERE, LIKE CARBON DIOXIDE, TRAP HEAT. THIS GREENHOUSE EFFECT PREVENTS THE SUN'S HEAT FROM ESCAPING. THIS WARMS EARTH.

WHAT IF YOU GOT SUCKED INTO A BLACK HOLE?

There are regions in space that are like hungry vacuum cleaners. They suck up everything in sight. Are you next?

COULD THIS REALLY HAPPEN?

NO WAY **HIGHLY UNLIKELY** ? MAYBE ABSOLUTELY

"You have to be close to a black hole to fall into one. The nearest one is about 3,000 light-years (17,000 trillion miles, or 28,000 trillion km) away. It is circling a dim orange star that it is slowly consuming."

—Dr. Mordecai-Mark Mac Low, Astrophysicist, American Museum of Natural History in New York City, New York

LOOK OUT BELOW

f you got sucked into a black hole, it would be a strange one-way trip. As you fall feetfirst toward the event horizon, the gravity pulling at you would be severe. It would pull on your feet more strongly than your head, stretching you out like a long, thin noodle. Scientists call this "spaghettification." But that's not all. Like all things that end up here, you'd be squeezed almost infinitely small. Ouch!

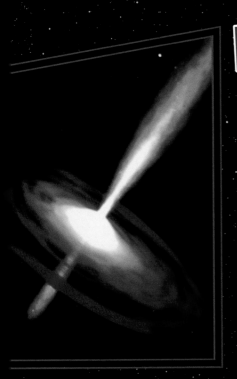

SAFETY SQUAD

Why aren't scientists worried that you'll wind up getting spaghettified? They've been on the lookout. Because black holes are invisible, the only way to detect them is by watching what's nearby.

"Black holes stretch and pull stars apart through spaghettification," explains Mac Low. "Whatever falls in gets squeezed hard enough to raise its temperature to a hundred million or a billion degrees." Anything that hot blazes in X-rays.

When you point an X-ray telescope at a black hole, the matter in the accretion disk glares brightly. This helps scientists spy where and how massive a black hole is. Lucky for you — and the future of humanity — there isn't one that will ever get close enough to suck you in.

THE WHOLE TRUTH ABOUT

BLACK HOLES

A black hole is a strange, invisible object. It's an object so dense and massive that the pull of its gravity is huge. Nothing that gets drawn too close can escape—not even light.

Where do these super suckers come from? Stars! You learned on page 23 that stars are born and die. When massive stars, ones much heftier than the sun, reach the end of their lives, they blow up.

This explosion is called a supernova. Material left behind collapses into itself. The more massive the leftovers, the more gravity it has. It keeps pulling itself inward until it becomes a black hole.

SUPER SUCKERS

Not all black holes are created equal. The Milky Way has a black hole four to six million times the **mass** of the sun at its center. Most other galaxies have black holes this large or even larger.

In 2012, astronomers spotted what may be the largest black hole in the universe. That giant has the mass of approximately 17 billion suns!

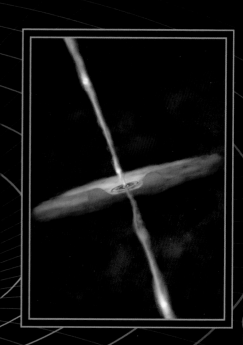

◆ MONSTER EATERS ◆

How do some black holes get so large? It takes millions of years for them to grow. They suck up anything nearby, including gas, dust, planets, and stars. "Stars fly around the black hole at the center of the Milky Way like a swarm of bees," says Mac Low. Some black holes can even suck up other black holes!

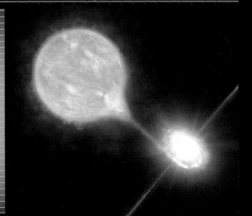

WATCH A BLACK HOLE IN ACTION!

Accretion Disk

As gas gets close to a black hole it goes into orbit here. The gas swirls among other caught gas in a Frisbee-like disk. This gas can still escape. That's if it can travel fast enough to fight the black hole's gravity.

Event Horizon

This is the point of no return. "Anything that tries to get out from within here is turned around by the black hole's gravity," says Mac Low.

Singularity

Gravity is so strong here that everything that falls in is crushed beyond recognition. Even the smallest particle of matter, an atom, would not survive here.

WHAT IF YOU WERE STRANDED ON MARS?

You're exploring Mars. Except you lost track of time and forgot to return to your spacecraft in time for liftoff. Oops. You're stranded! Will you survive?

COULD THIS REALLY HAPPEN?

NO WAY!
?

HIGHLY UNLIKELY   MAYBE   ABSOLUTELY

"Since we haven't sent anyone to Mars yet, the chance of getting stranded there is pretty low. Plus, we have good planning practices to ensure that that would never happen."

**—Jennifer Heldmann, Astrobiologist and Mars expert,
NASA's Ames Research Center in Mountain View, California**

WHAT'S UP WITH MARS?

Mars is the fourth planet from the sun. It is also one of Earth's closest neighbors. Humans have long wondered what it would be like to hop next door. NASA hopes to send the first astronauts around 2030. But in the meantime, scientists are figuring out ways to help humans survive on Mars.

WATCH OUT!

It's Dusty and Windy

Mars is covered in reddish, iron-rich dirt. That's why it's nicknamed the "red planet." Sometimes, giant storms can whip dust all over Mars. Some dust storms can rage at speeds up to 66 miles (106 km) per hour.

You'll Freeze and Burn

Mars has a very thin atmosphere. It can't trap enough solar energy to warm the planet. (Remember the diagram on page 22?) Mars averages a frigid −76 degrees Fahrenheit (−60°C)! At the same time, the thin atmosphere can't protect you from the sun's rays. Extreme exposure can harm the body by causing cancer, for example.

There's No Air or Water

Humans need to breathe and drink. There's barely any oxygen on Mars. As for water, scientists believe liquid water once flowed on Mars. Not today, though. Where did it go? "That's one of the outstanding questions," says Heldmann. "We know that there's frozen water on Mars." It's inside the ground and also frozen close to the surface near the poles. There is also a small amount of water vapor in the thin Martian atmosphere. A future NASA mission might help solve the mystery of where the liquid water went.

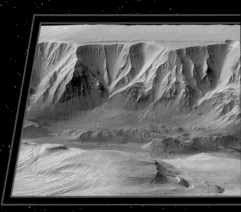

How will future Mars explorers withstand the brutal environment? One method is to dress properly. A space suit is designed to keep an astronaut's body safe and comfortable.

A "Mars suit" will need to, among other things, help block harmful solar **radiation**, feed oxygen for breathing, and keep the body at the right temperature. Space suits used today for working outside the International Space Station are too clunky for Mars. On Mars, astronauts need to climb around the planet's rocky setting. Scientists are now studying ways to make space suits that are light and flexible enough to move around in, says Heldmann.

PACK RIGHT

An astronaut also needs about 67 pounds (30 kg) of food, air, and water each day to survive. Mars is approximately 35 million miles (56 million km) away from Earth. Given the distance, they can't fly back and forth to pick up supplies. That makes tons of goods to jam into a spacecraft.

Scientists think building a greenhouse on Mars could help lighten the load. Here's how:

/FOOD/
INSTEAD OF BRINGING ALL THE FOOD FROM EARTH, FARM ON MARS! VEGETABLES, LIKE LETTUCE AND TOMATOES, ARE EASY TO GROW. THEY WOULD HELP PROVIDE ASTRONAUTS WITH FRESH FOOD.

/AIR/
PLANTS HAVE A FOOD-MAKING PROCESS CALLED PHOTOSYNTHESIS. THEY TAKE IN CARBON DIOXIDE GAS, THE MAIN GAS IN MARTIAN AIR, TO MAKE FOOD. THE PLANTS GIVE OFF OXYGEN IN RETURN. THAT'S WHAT HUMANS BREATHE!

/WATER/
THE WATER FROZEN IN THE GROUND CAN BE MELTED. ONCE CLEANED UP, ASTRONAUTS CAN USE IT TO WATER THE PLANTS, AND FOR DRINKING.

EXTREME MAKEOVER?

Would it ever be possible to live on Mars like you would on Earth? Maybe. Scientists have been thinking up ways to terraform the planet. That means to make it more Earthlike. How?

One idea is to pump gases into the air to create a greenhouse effect. The gases will bulk up the planet's thin atmosphere. This will trap heat from the sun, warming the planet. The increase in temperatures will help melt the water frozen in the ground. Then, "you could just walk outside, grow your carrots and lettuce, and live a regular life," says Heldmann.

GLOSSARY

Asteroid: a chunk of space rock that orbits the sun. It measures over 160 feet (49 m) wide, but is too small to be a planet.

Atmosphere: the blanket of gases that surrounds a planet or any other object in space

Friction: the slowing force caused by two objects rubbing against each other

Galaxy: a system of millions or billions of stars, along with the objects within it

Gravity: a pulling force that attracts one object to another

Mass: the amount of matter, or stuff, in an object

Meteor: a streak of light caused by a meteoroid as it plunges through Earth's atmosphere

Meteorite: a space rock that lands on Earth's surface

Meteoroid: a piece of space debris under 165 feet (50 m) wide. It can be as small as a piece of sand.

Microbe: a microscopic organism

Orbit: the path an object makes around another object

Photosynthesis: the process by which plants convert energy from sunlight into food

Radiation: energy transmitted through space as particles or waves

Satellite: a man-made spacecraft that orbits the Earth. Often they collect and send information that allows you to see pictures on your TV or receive a call on a cell phone.

Star: a large ball of gas that shines from its own energy

Universe: space and all the objects within it